T0107286

Supercharged
Goal Setting

Supercharged
Goal Setting

Warren Greshes

MEDIA

Published 2019 by Gildan Media LLC
aka G&D Media
www.GandDmedia.com

Front Cover design by David Rheinhardt of Pyrographx

Interior design by Meghan Day Healey of Story Horse, LLC

Library of Congress Cataloging-in-Publication Data is available upon request

ISBN: 978-1-7225-0023-8

10   9   8   7   6   5   4   3   2   1

CONTENTS

ONE

The Power of Commitment

When I first started speaking about commitment, I started to wonder, where does it all come from? What can we do to develop commitment?

The key to answering these questions is to look back at your own life, your own experiences, and your own turning points. We all have them, although we don't think we do. We always minimize our own experiences and the turning points in our lives, but when we look back, we find out that they're there.

That's what I did. I looked back at my life. I looked at what drives me every day, and all of a sudden it hit me. It all came back to a set of questions that were asked of me many years ago. Unfortunately for me, the true meaning of those questions did not sink in until almost eleven years later. But when it did, it changed the entire direction of my life. And when I look at, talk to, and read about all the successful people in this world, they seem to have the ability to answer that set of questions that was asked of me.

So let me go back to when I graduated from college in 1972. If I had been one-quarter as smart as I thought I was, I would have been really smart. But like so many other young people who graduate from college, I had no clue. None. Zip. Zero. I had no idea what I wanted to do with my life, no idea what I wanted to do with my career. I had spent four years majoring in snack bar.

You grow up your whole life, and everybody tells you, "You got to go to college."

"Why? Why do you got to go? Why?"

"You got to go."

"Why?"

"You got—you're going."

"All right, I'm going."

Then they tell you, "Remember: They can never take it away from you. When you've got that four-year degree, doors will just swing open."

Now I'm standing there with this four-year degree. I'm waiting: come on, start swinging. Nothing's happening. So I accepted an executive position at the local car wash. They made me the head wiper. I spent about four months working in this car wash after I graduated from college. I saved up all the money I could, and four months later, I put a pack on my back and I split. I left for Europe. like so many other young people back then.

The best thing I love about traveling through Europe is that you can move from country to country with the same ease with which we here move from state to state, because the countries are so small. But back in 1972, you still had to pass through customs. (Since then, the EU passed the Schengen Agreement, which more or less abolished border checks).

The story takes place on a train going from Paris to Munich, West Germany (yes, young people reading this, there was a West Germany). I'm on this train. All of a sudden the train stops. It's very early in the morning, about 5 a.m. I wake up and I'm groggy. As a recent college grad 5 a.m. was for coming home, not getting up. So I'm semicomatose and I wake up; I lift open the shade on the window. It's one of those dark, dreary, drizzly, foggy days, and we're on the West German border. As I look out through the fog and the mist, the only thing I can see is a group of West German border guards. I don't know if you've ever had the experience of coming in contact with West German border guards, but I can tell you, these were not the most fun guys in the world. They never smiled.

I'm just short of twenty-one. It's my first time ever outside the United States. I'm all by myself. It's early in the morning, I'm groggy, half asleep, looking into the fog and the mist at West German border guards. You know how you start to play up all these scenarios in your mind. The only thing I can think of is those old World War II movies that I grew up watching, where the border guards come on the train and ask to see your papers. They always ask for papers, and then they drag you off the train. They beat the crap out of you. They throw you by the side of the road, never to be heard from again.

I know I have nothing to worry about. I've done nothing wrong, but you can't help being a little paranoid in these situations.

All of a sudden these border guards come on the train. They start to grab passports and ask questions. They come to me. They grab my passport, they look at my passport, and they look at me. Again they look at my passport, and they look at me. Finally they ask me those questions—the questions that every single successful person can answer. The questions with true meaning. They did not sink until almost eleven years later, but when they did, it changed the entire direction of my life.

Those border guards asked me, "Where have you been? Why are you here? And where are you going?"

Unless you can answer those questions, unless you have a clear idea of where it is you want to end up and how you're going to get there, there's no way you can develop that sense of commitment or that burning desire to do whatever it takes to be the best. Because the key to success and the key to achievement is to have a sense of purpose and a goal. It is that sense of purpose, that goal, that gives us a reason to be committed to our own success.

You know what I find incredibly scary? The fact that only 5 percent of all the people out there actually have goals. You know what's even scarier? Only 1 percent ever write them down. You know the single biggest reason that people do not get what they want out of life? They never bother to figure out what it is. If you don't know what you want, how are you going to get it? And if you don't know what you want, how you know you don't already have it? You couldn't recognize what it was, so you just let it pass you by.

You may laugh, but how many people do we know that have passed up all the greatest opportunities in their lives because they didn't recognize them? They didn't know what they were looking for, and they just saw it pass them by. When it was too late, they recognized that that was what they wanted out of their lives, and it was gone.

You ask most people what they want out of their lives and they talk in vagaries. They say things like, "I want to make a lot of money."

"That's good. What's a lot of money?"

Or they'll say, "Oh, I want a better job."

"Better than what?"

"Better than what I have."

"How much better? A little bit? A lot? Less than a bit?"

"I want a bigger house. I want a nicer car. I want more. I want a lot."

"What does that mean?"

What's a lot of money? I ask people that question all the time. They always give me vague answers, and they always take money out of the air. It's not a matter of what it is, it's a matter of what it's going to do for you. Because understand something about money: money is a vehicle. That's all it is. Money is a vehicle that allows you to live the lifestyle that you want to live. So what you really need to know is the type of lifestyle you want to live. You have to be able to define how you want your life to look. Once you've defined it, that will tell you how much money you need to support it.

Most people give me all sorts of sums, but if you don't know what you're going to do with the money, what's the motivation for getting it? There isn't any. Money is not a motivator. No one ever gets up in the morning and says, "I just can't wait to get to work today because they pay me well."

No one ever says that. People do say things like, "I really hate this job. Man, I want to get a better job. I can't stand this place. I'd love to get out of here, but you know what? This is all I know. What else can I do? Besides, they pay me pretty well, so I might as well stay."

Whoa. Talk about commitment. "They pay me pretty well, so I might as well stay."

Have you ever worked at a job you hated? Did you ever have an occasion to get a raise on that job? Yes, you did. The day after you got the raise, you came to work. Did you still hate the job? You still hated the job just as much if not more. Right after the day they gave you a raise, the money meant nothing. It didn't make you any happier. It didn't make you any more productive.

Money is not the motivator; it's what the money can do for us that motivates us. That's why people give out all these numbers. I'll ask most people, "What's a lot of money?" Single guys usually say a million dollars; for some reason, single guys always say a million dollars. When I ask them what they're going to do with it, they always say the same thing: they're going to buy a Porsche. I guess they figure that'll make it easier to be going around meeting women or something, I don't know. But they all say they're going to buy a Porsche.

I say to them, "Let me ask you a question. Do you need a million dollars to buy a Porsche?"

"No."

"What do you need?"

"You need, like, $100,000."

"But do you really? Do you really need $100,000? If you really wanted a Porsche, couldn't you just lease it? What do you need? Nothing. You don't need a down payment. You don't need anything. Do you have nothing today?"

They always say, "Oh, yeah."

"Then how come you don't have a Porsche?"

Maybe because it's not what they really wanted. Understand something about *a lot*. Everybody's *a lot* is different. It's OK; it does not matter what your *a lot* is. You know what matters? That *you* know what it is. Because unless you know what it is, how are you going to formulate a plan to get it? And if you don't know what it is, how do you know you don't already have it?

About five years ago, I was doing a seminar in New York City. I was going around the audience asking, "Give me a definition of success."

One young man in the audience said, "Money."

I said, "What do you mean by money? Do you mean a lot of money?"

"Yeah," he said.

"So what's a lot of money?"

He said, "Whatever will make me comfortable."

I said, "What will make you comfortable?"

He said, "Whatever will get me everything I want."

So, I asked, "What do you want?"

He said, "A lot of money."

Now we're going around this circle for what seems like a day or two. Finally I say to this guy, "Look, pal. Give me a number. Something. What's a lot?"

He said, "Eighty billion dollars."

Now I had to admit, that's a lot. But watch what happened next.

"OK," I said. "You got it. You've got the $80 billion. What are you going to do with it?"

He said, "I'm going to spend it."

He must have thought he was a Congressman.

"What are you going to spend it on?" I said.

He said, "I'm going to buy everything."

At this point, I was doing the same thing you're doing. I was trying to conceive a picture in my mind of how someone does that. How do you buy everything? You know the only thing I could come up with? You know those supermarket sweeps programs on cable? So I said to him, "What are you going to do? You going to back up a truck to Macy's and say, 'Give me everything'?"

"No, you don't understand."

Right, like I'm the one who's crazy.

"I'm going to buy the United States," he said.

"Stop. Stop right there," I said. "Could you buy the United States for $80 billion?"

"No."

"Well, then, is that a lot of money?"

"I guess not."

You see, it's only a lot if it's going to get you what you want. But if you don't know what you want, then how do you know what you have to do to get it? And if you don't know what it is, how do you know you don't already have it?

Knowing what you want and having goals are not necessarily the same thing. Knowing what you want is good. You have to know what you want in order to set the goal. But how do we recognize an opportunity unless we first decide, in our minds and on paper, what that opportunity looks like? That's why people miss all the opportunities in their lives: when it showed up, they didn't know it was an opportunity. They finally figured out it was an opportunity after the opportunity was gone. The world is filled with people who have war stories of all the great things they could have done with their lives if only they had been smart enough to take advantage of the opportunity the second it hit. They were smart enough, they just didn't bother to figure out what that opportunity was going to look like. You know what's even more amazing about those people? Many times they actually get what they wanted out of life, but because they never bothered to figure out what it is and they've never been able to describe it, they just let it pass them by, because they don't recognize it as the opportunity they've been waiting for their entire lives.

It's sad how many people believe that they're not going to get what they want out of life. They believe, "Oh, I could never hope to be like that. I could never hope to be that rich. I could never hope to have that kind of a life."

Ever hear this? "The only way I'm ever going to get something like that is if I win the lottery." I hate that. I hate lotteries. Well, I hate them and I love them. I hate them because I think they're nothing more than an education tax on people who can't afford it. But I love them because, since I never enter them, everybody is paying my education tax for me.

It's incredible how we've conditioned people to believe that the lottery is something they should be shooting for. It's incredible, because you ain't going to win. The odds in New York State are 12 million to one. You ain't going to win. But there are people who bank all their dreams on it.

Many years ago, the top prize in New York State was $20 million. People were in line all around the streets for tickets. The media love this stuff. They trot out the TV cameras, and they interview all these people. They always ask them the same stupid questions. They say, "What are you going to do with the money?"

I will never forget watching this. One woman said, "I'm going to travel around the world." Another woman said, "I'm going to buy my mother a house." Some guy said, "I'm going to pay off my debts." I'm watching this and asking myself, what kind of debts could this guy have? Could you imagine his Mastercard bill?

Then I thought, "Hold it. Hey, lady, do you need $20 million to travel around the world? Hey, lady, is your mother's house really going to cost $20 million? Hey pal, do you need $20 million to pay off your debts? What's going to happen when you don't win? Because you're not going to win."

I thought about this. The day after those numbers are pulled, what's going to happen to these three people? Is this woman never going to travel around the world? Is that other woman never going to buy her mother a house? Is this guy never going to pay off his debts? If I were watching that show and I were one of his creditors, I'd be knocking on his door right away, because he ain't going to win. When they don't win, are they just going to give up their life's dreams? Are their whole life's dreams contingent on a 12 million-to-one shot?

Is this what we've come to? Don't they always ask you, "Will you quit your job?" As if that is the absolute best thing you could do—stop working. Because let's face it: what defines us more than our work? When we first meet each other, what do we always ask?

"What do you do?"

"Oh, me, I sit around."

I love those commercials of the guy sitting there fishing in a rowboat. That looks like fun. Boy, that looks like something I want to do every single day for the rest of my life.

A few months later, there was a $26 million prize, and it was won by a Nigerian exchange student. This guy was on TV. The lights were all around him, and they were interviewing him, and they were saying, "Boy, this is great." And it was; I was happy for him. You win $26 million; it's great; there's nothing wrong with it. But they asked him his feelings. You know what he said? "This is great. This could only happen in America."

When I heard that, I said, "Wow, that's a real compliment." I always thought the American dream was something a lot different than that. The American dream still brings people here from all over the world. I always thought the American dream was that you could come here, you could do whatever you want, and if you worked as hard as you wanted, if you tried as hard as you could, you could make anything you wanted out of your life. I always thought that was the dream.

You see what we're changing the dream to? We're telling people that the best thing that could ever happen to you is to win the lottery. All I could think of was a group of people in some foreign country, sitting around the table and saying things like, "Listen, folks, if we pick number three, eighteen, twenty-six, forty-two, forty-eight, fifty-four, we go to America, we spend a buck, and we get out of there." Boy, that's something to be proud of.

According to CNBC, in 2017 there were more than 11 million households in the US whose net worth was $1 million or more, not including their primary residence. Eleven million millionaires, which meant one out of almost every 10 households in this country had a net worth of a million or more, and over 75 percent of those millionaires were self-made.

Let me tell you something else. When they surveyed those self-made millionaires, you know what the secrets were? Sense of purpose, goals, plans, a commitment to excellence, efforts, hard work, smart work. In other words, what they're saying is this: if you know what you want and you have a commitment to going out there and getting it and working hard to get it, you've got a one in 10 chance. Not bad.

On the other hand, the State of New York will tell you that all you need is a dollar and a dream, and you've got a 12 million to one chance. Ten to one; 12 million to one—the choice is up to you. The state of New York says all you need is a dollar and a dream. Warren Greshes says keep your buck. Save it. Invest it in your future. Because all you really need is a dream.

TWO

Why They Don't Do It

I want to talk about why people don't do all the things they know they should do. I've talked about commitments. I've talked about setting goals, about the importance of having a sense of purpose in your life. I've always notice that when I talk about this stuff, people sit in the audience, and their heads are all bobbing up and down, like the little doll in the back of the window of the car: "Oh, yeah, he's right. Oh, yeah, I know that. Oh, yeah, you know, I've heard that a million times. This is nothing new. Absolutely; that's what you've got to do."

If you know I'm right, if you know it's got to be done, if you know it's the right thing to do, if you've heard it a million times, then how come you don't do it?

Why don't people do it? I want to explore the two biggest reasons people don't do all the things they know they should.

The first one obviously is fear—fear of failure. The single biggest reason that people do not succeed is they are afraid to fail. Fear of failure is the single biggest obstacle to success.

We've been taught to believe it's not OK to be afraid. Let me tell you something right up front. It's OK to be afraid.

You know what's not OK? To let the fear stop you.

Everybody's afraid. Change is scary. No one likes change. No one likes the unknown. Heading into the unknown is a scary thought, it's a scary task, and it's natural to be afraid. But it's not good to let the fear stop you.

Many years ago, I was giving a talk to a group of MBA candidates at New York University. We were talking about all sorts of business topics, motivational topics, and near the end of my talk, a young man raised his hand and asked me, "When you started your business and you wrote your business plan, what was your contingency for failure?"

Typical MBA question, right? I looked him right in the eye and said, "There was none, because failure never crossed my mind."

Why would I do it if I even thought about failing? Why would I even attempt to start my own business saying, "Well, just in case I fail . . ."? That's like a self-fulfilling prophecy. But how many people do that in their lives? How many people attempt to change their lives by holding on to something they want to let go of? How many people enter a business and say, "If I fail, I can always go back to my old job"?

"Well, yeah—marriage is a scary step, but I figure if it doesn't always work out, I can always get a divorce." That's some way to go through marriage. That's some way to go through business: "If my new job doesn't work out, I can always go back to the old place that I hated so much that I couldn't stand to get up in the morning." You see what you're doing? Before you even start on the journey, you're already convincing yourself that it's not going to work.

There was absolutely no contingency for failure, as far as I was concerned. Failure never crossed my mind. Was I afraid? Sure, I was afraid. Was I afraid I was going to fail? No, I was just afraid of something new. Failure never crossed my mind. Why? Because I planned it out. I knew what I was going to do. I spent years polishing my craft. I knew I could sell. I knew I could bring in clients. That's the most important thing—bringing in business. There's an old equation: if you have no clients, you ain't in business. But I knew I could do that. There was no fear involved in that. I was not afraid.

I hate it when I hear people say, "I'll keep my regular job, and I'll do this part-time. If it works out, I'll leave my job." You can't be successful part-time. Successful people are not successful part of the time; successful people are successful all of the time. You cannot cross to the other side of the river if you keep one foot on the side that you're starting out on.

I remember playing on those hand-over-hand bars in the park when I was a kid. You know: You can't get there if you keep one hand stuck on the first bar. You have to let go of that first bar. But the fear of failure, the fear that we're going to fall, stops us because we've been conditioned to think failure's a terrible thing. We've been conditioned to think that falling down is a terrible thing. Falling down is not a terrible thing. What's a terrible thing is not getting up. It doesn't matter how times you fall if you keep getting up.

Remember: successful people do all the things that unsuccessful people are unwilling to do. You've got to be willing to break away from the pack. You've got to be willing to do things that everybody else is not willing to do. You've got to be willing to be different if you want to be successful in life, in your career. You've got to be willing to separate yourself from your competition. Why should I deal with you if you're just like everybody else?

People amaze me. I can set my watch by the human race. The highways are crowded the same exact time every single day. And what do they do? They sit in their cars in traffic and scream and yell to themselves how much they hate the highway. "I hate this road. Oh, man, this road is always so crowded every single day. I can't stand it. I hate sitting in this traffic." What do they do the next day? Same thing. Same exact road, same exact time, same exact traffic, same exact complaint.

You know what, folks? In most cases, all you've got to do is make that tiny little change. Small changes implemented on a consistent basis will always yield you great results. Maybe leave fifteen or twenty minutes earlier in the morning. Maybe go home fifteen or twenty minutes later at night. But no, most people will sit in traffic and complain about it.

People are so resistant to change. They're so afraid of what might happen. We've been conditioned to think that failure is such a terrible thing. So what? It's just another experience in your life. We value our experiences; we learn from our experiences. But we're always told, don't step out of the way, don't do anything different, don't try to go beyond the crowd.

Ever go to the movies? If you ever go to one of those places, they're all the same. They all have four or five sets of double glass doors. Do you ever watch when the crowd files out? You have four or five sets of double glass doors, so you have eight to ten doors. None of them is locked, but only one is swung open—the one all the way to the right. Two hundred people file out of the movie theater, and they all go for this one little opening on the right, and they're all trying to squeeze through.

All you'd have to do to break away from the crowd is take one little extra step to the left and exert some effort. It's that way in life. Just break away and exert some effort. But most people don't do it. Why? "Well, if I break away from the crowd, what if I push the door and it's locked?" Oh, heavens, well, kill yourself. What do you mean, what do you do? Try another door. Because if all you choose to do with your life is follow the crowd, all you can ever hope to be is one of the crowd.

We've always been told that if we fall down, that's the worst thing that could possibly happen to us. No. The worst thing that could possibly happen to us is that we don't get up. We've been so conditioned to believe that failure is terrible. No, it's not. And you don't fail if you keep going. You only fail when you stop.

Did you fail your driving test on the first go-around? (I learned to drive in New York City. In New York, they pass you according to how many people you hit.) A lot of people failed their driving test the first time around. What do they do? They keep taking the test until they finally pass it, and then they get their license. Why do we keep calling that failure? That's not failure. That's falling down.

It never ceases to amaze me how we just put the tag of failure on these things. Most adults will fail, fall down, and not pick themselves up. Only the successful ones will keep going. Isn't that an incredible attitude? You don't fail if you keep getting up.

Don't be afraid, folks. Don't be afraid to fail. It's OK to fail. It's just not OK if you let the fear and the failure stop you.

Now let's look at the second thing that stops more people from being successful than anything else. Very simply, that's all those little things you know you should do but don't. It's all those little things that we just can't seem to change. Procrastination.

We just can't seem to get out of bed at certain times. We just can't seem to get going every day. We just can't seem to get that paperwork done. We just can't seem to make those calls.

What are those really? Habits—all those conditioned habits that we've developed over the years that stop us from being successful. You know why people don't change habits? Not because we don't want to. We all want to. It's not a matter of wanting to or not wanting to. We don't change habits simply because of the way we go about doing it.

There's a difference between a habit and an addiction like smoking, drinking, or drug use. The only way, or the most successful way, to cure an addiction is very simply blam—cold turkey. You've just got to stop. If you have ever quit smoking, you know it is extremely difficult, almost impossible, to quit by cutting back. The easiest and fastest way to quit smoking is to just stop doing it, cold turkey.

I used to smoke. I used to try to quit by cutting back. I was one of those people that said, "I can quit whenever I want; I've done it a million times." I used to do the old cut-back method: "I'm only going to smoke one cigarette an hour." You smoke a cigarette and then you sweat for fifty-three minutes. Right? You sit there staring at your watch going, "Come on . . ."

No, you've got to cut it out. It's the only way to stop an addiction. You can't say, "I used to drink two bottles a day, but now I'm no longer an alcoholic. I'm cured. I only drink one bottle a day." You're still an alcoholic. AA will tell you that. One day at a time, but you've got to stop.

The way you change a habit is the opposite of the way you change an addiction. Most people try to change a habit cold turkey—by stopping. But the only way to change a habit is a little bit at a time, because that's the way you acquired it.

That's the problem: we try to change our addictions by cutting back, but we try to change our habits by going cold turkey. People say to me, "I've been procrastinating for years, but I'm going to change. Monday morning I'm going to come into work with lists, and I'm going to get all my paperwork done the second I touch it. Every piece of paper I touch for the first time, I'm going to get it taken care of. I'm going to go from being the world's greatest procrastinator on Friday to being the world's most organized person on Monday."

And I say, "Forget it. You can't do it." Because if you try to go from one end of the spectrum to the other in one shot, what's going to happen? The change is so drastic that you're going to hate it, and you're going to give up.

It's like losing weight. Everybody figures they've got to lose all the weight all at once, because they believe that's the way they put it on. They didn't. The only way to lose weight is a little bit at a time, because that's how they gained it. Ninety-seven percent of the people who lose weight gain it back and more because of the way they lose it.

You know these crazy diets—they don't work. You know why? Because the change is too drastic. People go on these crazy diets and decide, "I've got to lose twenty-one pounds. I've got to lose twenty-one pounds in thirteen days, so I'm going to go on the grapefruit and dust diet. That's it. I'll eat nothing but grapefruit and dust for thirteen days." You eat grapefruit and dust for thirteen days and you do—you lose the twenty-one pounds. After thirteen days of eating nothing but grapefruit and dust, what are you going to do? You're going to go nuts, you're going to have a potato-chip frenzy. Right?

Then there are those crazy diets where you can only eat one thing. Oh, a delicious shake for breakfast, a delicious shake for lunch. Come on, people—how are you going to eat a shake for breakfast and a shake for lunch every day for the rest of your life without wanting to kill somebody? You'll walk past the pizza place and you'll eat them out of business because the change is so terrible. How do you feel about dieting? You hate it. You hate it so much you're not going to do it.

My favorite is when people say to me, "I have so much trouble getting up in the mornings. I just can't roll out of bed. I want to get up early. I want to read the newspaper. I'm going to work out, I'm going to eat breakfast, I'm going to get my paperwork done, I'm going to get to the office. I just can't get out of bed."

"Well, what time do you get out of bed in the morning?"

"Oh, man, by the time I roll out of bed it's always 9:30."

"What time do you set your alarm for?"

"Five."

Five! You know those people who hit the snooze alarm every seven or eight minutes for the next four hours? Do you know how tiring it is to sleep in eight-minute intervals?

And I go, "Are you nuts?"

"You don't understand. I want to read the papers every morning, and I want to eat breakfast, and I want to run four miles."

"Yes, but you're getting up at 9:30."

"But I want to get up at 5."

"You can't. You can't make that kind of drastic change."

"Well, how can I do it?"

"You can do it like this. Can you get up at 9:15?"

"Sure."

"Tomorrow, set your alarm for 9:15. When it goes off, get out of bed. Now that's not what you wanted, but it's fifteen minutes better than you've been doing. You do that for a month. And you know what? Next month set your alarm at 9. When it goes off, get out of bed. Do that for another month. Then set your alarm at 8:45, and when it goes off, get out of bed. Do that for another month, then, 8:30. Just keep doing that."

The whole key to changing habits is to always remember: a little bit a lot rather than a lot a little bit.

THREE
The Five Levels of Success

What is success? And what are some of the things we should be looking at? What things should we should be going after? How do we define success? Is everything just based on money? Is all our success, are all our goals monetary goals?

No. Absolutely not. The true definition of success says that you must be able to create a balance in your life. To be truly successful, you must be able to reach a high level of happiness in more than one area. Because it's not all just money.

A lot of us have been led to believe that in the past. Throughout the eighties, we were told that if you had money, you were automatically a success. People were held up to us as these great successes. Why—simply because they accumulated a lot of money? If you want to tell me that money is simply equated with success and that the successful people in the world are the ones that have the most money, then I'll tell you that you consider drug dealers successful, because, after all, they have a lot of money. If that's the case, then they're the successes in the world. But I don't think you really believe that.

In order to be truly successful, you must reach a high level of happiness in a number of different areas. You must create that balance in your life. That's what we've learned from the last decades. We've learned that the really successful people are the ones that have found that balance, are the ones that have found that lifestyle, are the ones that are happy at a number of different levels.

I want to talk about the five different levels of success—the five different areas of concentration where you need to create a high level of happiness in order to be truly successful. And I want to tell you right now that there is no one area that's more important than the other. They're all equally important.

FINANCIAL HAPPINESS

The first area of concentration where you need to achieve a high level of happiness is what I call *financial happiness*. What is financial happiness? Does that mean you make a lot of money? Not necessarily. Financial happiness means that you earn the amount of money you need to support the lifestyle you want to live.

So what we really need to know is, what kind of lifestyle do we want to live? That will tell us the amount of money we need. Not everybody has the same kind of lifestyle. Some people choose to live a modest lifestyle. Some people choose to live a lavish lifestyle. There are people who enjoy going camping when they go on vacation. Other people enjoy going to four-star hotels. What's the difference? It's what you enjoy, not what somebody else enjoys. That will determine whether you have reached financial happiness or not.

I'm talking about the people who truly don't need a lot of money to live on. I know someone like that, one of the happiest people I know. He's a garbage man for the city of New York. If you ask him what he does for a living, he tells you he's a doctor of garbology. He is the happiest guy I know. You see him and you ask him how he's doing, he always says, "Fantastic." And you have to believe him, because he's got a twenty-inch neck and he'll snap you like a twig if you don't. But I've never met somebody that can make collecting garbage sound so exciting. He just loves doing it. He loves his lifestyle. He makes the amount of money he needs to support his family in the way he wants to and the way they want to live. They do the things they want. They do the things they like.

He says, "Oh, I love collecting garbage." I say, "Why?" He says, "I like working outdoors." To me, working outdoors is being a forest ranger, not a garbage man. But he loves it. So who am I to say? He's doing what he wants to do. He is living the lifestyle he wants to live, and he's making the amount of money he needs to live that lifestyle. That's true financial happiness. It doesn't matter what your lot is. It only matters that you know what it is.

CAREER HAPPINESS

Let's go to number two, which I call *career happiness*. What does career happiness mean? It means that you work at a job that you truly love. If you've ever worked a job you hated, you know that it's a total mental prison.

In order to be successful, you have to love what you do. There's no choice, because in order to be successful in a career, in business, you have to be willing to put in an inordinate amount of time, energy, effort, and commitment toward it. If you don't like it, you're not going to be willing to do it. That's one reason I changed careers. I used to work in the garment center in New York City. Why did I change careers? Because I hated it. Not because I wasn't making money; I was making pretty good money. But as I've already said, money's not a motivator.

I left that job, I changed careers, because I knew I could never be as successful as I really, truly wanted to be. Because I hated it. And because I hated it, I wasn't willing to put in the time it would take to be truly successful in this job.

I knew I had to find something I loved. I knew that if I did, I'd be willing to put in the time to be successful. Let's face it: change is scary. People work in jobs they hate because they don't want to change. Even though they hate it, at least they know it. At least they know what they're going into every single day.

Change is scary. I'm not going to minimize it. Sure, it's scary, but a lot of people rationalize it away by saying,

by 8:30. He's got to drive forty-five minutes just to get to the railroad station. He's got to leave work at 4:30 just to be home by 8:00 at night. I read this, and I said, "When does he see the birds? When does he see the trees? It's always dark. How does he know they're there? He didn't skip the rat race, he just made it worse."

Remember: when you want to be a forty-hour-a-week worker—if your attitude is "I get in at 9:00 and get the heck out of there at 5:00, and I don't care about anything else"—a forty-hour-a-week worker equals one thing: survival. That's the best you can hope to do. The best you can ever hope to do by putting in forty hours a week is getting by. It's the people that put in those extra five, ten, fifteen, twenty hours per week that become successful, because when you put in that extra time, that's an investment in your future.

As I read this, I thought, "This guy's boxed himself in a corner. Here's a guy that's willing to put in a fifteen-hour day. The problem is, seven of it is commuting. Why didn't this guy ever take a step back and say, 'I'm willing to put in a long day. Where I was, I was commuting an hour each way. If I put in a thirteen-hour day, I'd get an extra two hours of sleep. If I'm willing to commute an hour each way, I'll put in a thirteen-hour day; that means I'm working eleven hours.'" If he just worked eleven hours a day for a few years, maybe he could have afforded the house he wanted in the place he wanted to be in.

In the last few years, real-estate values have gone down in that area. But now he's locked into a forty-hour week. He can't work any more than that, because he's got to be commuting for seven. So here's a guy who has locked himself into survival at a young age, because he wasn't willing to take that step back to look long-range, to set a long-range goal.

You always have to look long-term. You can't make your decisions based on short-term implications. One of the best things you can do when it's time to make a decision is say, "If this were a perfect world and money were no object, what would I do?" That will help you decide what to do with your life.

That's career happiness: finding something you really, truly love. Finding something that makes you want to go to work every day. The money is not the motivator. When you're really doing something you love, you don't ever want to stop doing it. That's career happiness.

FAMILY HAPPINESS

Number three is what I call *family happiness*. What is family happiness? Does that mean you're married and you have children? Not necessarily. But it does mean that you know you cannot do it alone. You cannot be successful all on your own. That "pull yourself up by your own bootstraps" theory is good, but it doesn't go far enough, because you need help.

Everybody needs the support and help of other people to make it. No one makes it on their own. Whether it be your spouse, whether it be close friends, whether it be other people at work, you need to have a core of people that you can always count on when you need them, and in turn they know they can always count on you when they need you. That is true family happiness.

When people are about to make a career change, start a new job, or go into their own business, I always tell them one thing, especially if they're married: "Your first and most important sale is at home. If you can't close the sale at home, don't bother, because you're going to need that support."

If you're going to start a new job, if you're going to start a new career, if you're going to start a new business, you'd better get 2000 percent backing at home, because the world's going to be rough to you when you first start out, and when you come home, you don't need it to be rougher. You need that support at home.

I was very lucky. Thirty-three years ago, when I made the decision to start my own business, I went home and talked to my wife about it. I walked in and said to her, "I've decided I'm going into business for myself." Most of the time you hear things like, "Are you sure this is the right time?" or "Can we afford this now?" or "Did you think this thing through?" or "It sounds like a good idea. Tell me more about it." My wife looked me right in the eye, and all she said was, "It's about time."

What could stop me when you've got that kind of support? How can you be stopped? You can't. Yes, the change is scary, but you're always going to need that support. You'd better have that support at home. You can't do it alone.

Also, bring that person into the process. One of the first things I did when I started my own business was to take my wife with me on a road trip, a particularly rough one. We drove about 120 miles, and we stayed overnight in a crappy motel. I mean, crappy. If this place was ten times better, it would have been garbage.

The next morning, I did a full-day seminar. I finished speaking for a full day, hopped in the car, drove another fifty miles, and did a dinner talk. I finished that dinner talk about 10:00 or 10:30 at night, got back in the car, and drove all the way home, about another 100 miles. The next morning my wife woke up and said, "All I did is sit in the audience and I'm exhausted. I can't imagine how you feel." But that gave her a really good understanding of what I do and what's going on when I'm out there late and I'm working every single day.

Bring your spouse into the process if you need that support. Take them out on some appointments with you. Let them see what it is you do. Let them see that you're out there working; you're not sitting in some coffee shop somewhere.

You need that support, because when you come home after a rough day, you're going to need somebody in your corner 2000 percent. That's true family happiness.

The other part of family happiness is at work. You think you do it alone. No, you don't do it alone. Everybody in your office needs everybody else. I don't care how big or how small the link in that chain is. You break it—there ain't no chain.

Back in the 1970's, when I worked in the garment center, we had a head bookkeeper who was like most head bookkeepers. She had studied at the Attila the Hun school of head bookkeeping, and she was the worst. We had a shipping room from which we used to ship the dresses, and the people that worked in the shipping room were minimum-wage employees. Half of them were illegal immigrants. You didn't get top-quality people working in the shipping room.

We had one guy who was the invoice clerk: we called him the charge clerk. All he did all day was hand-write invoices. I was shipping out thousands of dresses a month. We probably shipped out about 15,000 dresses a month, and he'd stand there all day in his dusty, dirty, smelly shipping room, writing out invoices all day. The most boring job you can think of. He was in one spot the whole day.

Now this guy rarely made a mistake, but whenever he did, boy, oh boy, that head bookkeeper would jump on it. She would run into my office with that invoice, she'd throw it on my desk, and she'd go, "Here—look at this. What did I tell you about those people?"

Finally one day I'd had it. She came in with one of those invoices and said, "Here." I looked at her and said, "Sylvia, you're absolutely right. They're no good. So tell you what we're going to do. Right now, I'm going to walk downstairs to that shipping room, and I'm going to fire everybody."

She was looking at me like I was crazy. I said, "No, don't worry, Sylvia. It's OK. Because even if I fire them, understand something, me and you, we're geniuses, right? We're high-paid geniuses. We never make a mistake. I know you never do. So at 5:30, when the day is done, me and you, we're going to go down to the shipping room, and we'll do all the shipping and invoicing ourselves. What do you say, Sylvia?" That was the last I ever heard from her.

You need other people. I don't care who you are. I don't care what you do. I don't care how successful you are, have ever been, or will ever be. You need help. Once you start to understand that, once you start to understand that you can't do it alone, that you need that core around you that you can always count on and who can always count on you, then you've achieved family happiness.

MENTAL, EMOTIONAL, AND PHYSICAL HAPPINESS

The fourth area that I want to talk about is *mental, emotional, and physical happiness*. This is pretty self-explanatory. It means you're healthy. It means you have your peace of mind. That's very important.

There was a big burst of entrepreneurship in the eighties, and people were starting up businesses left and right, women especially. In fact, surveys showed that women were starting up businesses three to four times faster than men.

When they did surveys of female entrepreneurs to find out why they were starting these businesses, you know what they found out? That money had nothing to do with it. Maybe 1 or 2 percent of them said money. It was so far down the list, it was ridiculous. They wanted control. They wanted peace of mind. They wanted the ability to achieve and to be as successful as they could possibly be.

Because, let's face it, corporate America has the glass ceiling over their heads. In corporate America, many women can't rise above a certain level, so these women were saying, "I want to rise as far as my talent and my ability will take me, so I'll start my own business." Or "I want to be able to live the lifestyle I want to live. I have children. I want to be able to have a career and see my kids at the same time, so I'll start my own business and let my kids sit in the office. I want to have control over my life. I want to have control over my creativity. I want to have control over my ability." That's why they started businesses.

That's why most entrepreneurs started businesses. It's why I started mine. Not because of money, but because I wanted to be able do what I wanted to do when I wanted to do it. I wanted control. I wanted freedom. Money is not the motivator for most entrepreneurs. A lot of them start their businesses because they have a great idea and they want to fill a need that they perceive that society has. The money is just a by-product of your attitude, of your commitment, and of your action. That's what true mental and physical happiness is. That's where it comes from. That's why people do the things they do—for that peace of mind.

That's what's happening now. How many business magazines have you read where people are not going on the fast track anymore, because they realize that there was not that much to it? *Fortune* and *Business Week* have done a number of articles on it—how people are taking lateral moves within their companies because they want to be able to spend more time with their families. They want to be able to change their lifestyle. They're more interested in lifestyle now than they are in the fast track. They've found that they worked hard for the fast track and there was something missing. They didn't have that sense of balance, they didn't have that sense of control, and they want that now. That's mental and physical happiness.

SPIRITUAL HAPPINESS

Let's go to the fifth area of concern. It's called *spiritual happiness*. What does that mean? Does that mean you're a religious person? It could, but it doesn't necessarily.

Spiritual happiness means that you have a true sense of who you are. You have a true sense of your own self-worth, your own identity, and you feel that you make a difference. That you make a positive impact on people's lives and if you were not around, it would leave a void. That's very important to understand.

A lot of people have real problems in their lives because they never understand that. They never feel that they're making a difference. That's another reason I changed careers. I felt I wasn't making a difference. I was sitting there saying, "What does it matter if anybody buys these ugly dresses?" In fact, I started to feel I would be doing the world a service if I *didn't* sell anyone these dresses. Who wanted to watch women walking around in that garbage?

That's when I knew I had to get out, because I really felt I had the ability to make a difference in this world. That's why I do this, because I know that when I do, I have the ability to change people's lives in a positive way. I have the ability to make an impact. But you really have to feel that. You really have to understand that you do make a difference.

There was a book written called *When All You've Ever Wanted Isn't Enough* by Rabbi Harold Kushner. He talks about surveys done of middle-aged men who ended up in therapy. He looked at men from all walks of life, from rich men, industrialists, down to poor men—a wide cross-section. The single biggest reason they ended up in therapy was they didn't feel they were making a difference. They didn't feel they were making a positive impact on people's lives.

There's a movie I'm sure most of you know: *It's a Wonderful Life*. If you haven't seen it, you don't own a television set. If you own a television set, and you turn it on anytime between November 1 and the day after Christmas, you're forced to watch it.

Anyway, that movie was about spiritual happiness. Jimmy Stewart played a fellow named George Bailey. George Bailey lived in this "crummy little town" called Bedford Falls. He wanted to do great things. He wanted to travel the world, build things, do great things for people, but because of family circumstances, he got stuck in that crummy little town running the family business.

Remember the family business? The crummy little Bailey Building and Loan? They were building middle-class, single-family homes. He 's stuck in Bedford Falls running that crummy little building and loan. Then he gets into some serious financial trouble because of his drunken Uncle Billy, and he decides everybody would be better off if he killed himself.

So George Bailey decides to commit suicide, but since it's the movies, he has a guardian angel who says, "It's really stupid to kill yourself." And George says, "You're right. Probably everybody would have been better off if I had never been born."

Of course, again, since it's the movies, and you've got a guardian angel, you get to see what would have happened to you if you'd never been born. George finds that while he might not have done some of the great things he wanted to do, other people, because they had come in contact with him, had gone on to do great things. He had changed the course of people's lives through the impact he made on them.

The angel says, "It's amazing how many other people's lives we touch." We never think about that, do we? We never take that step back and think about how many other people's lives we touch.

In one of the last lines in the movie, George's brother toasts him: "To my brother, George, the richest man in town." The whole town came by, and everyone gave him money.

That's true spiritual happiness—the sense that you really do make a difference. That you do touch other people's lives in a positive way, and that if you weren't around, it would have left a void.

HOLDING THE BALANCE

What is true success? True success is when we can reach a high level of happiness in all five of these areas, and we can create that balance in our lives. If we let any one of those five get out of whack, it could drag the other four down with it.

Think about it. Have you ever known anybody who made a lot of money, had a fantastic career, owned a big business, and all of a sudden one day went through a terrible family problem, like a divorce? A really rough divorce or a bad custody case? Haven't you always found that it dragged down all the other areas of their lives, that everything just kind of fell apart? One terrible thing happens to someone, and things fall apart. One thing like that could drag everything else down.

Say you have young children. Have you ever gone to work on a day when one of your kids was home sick with something minor, like a twenty-four-hour virus? Is your mind fully on your work that day? No way. Your mind is partly at home. In fact, you probably called home twelve or fourteen times. You probably called and said to your kid, "Were you sleeping?"

"I was until you called again."

You see what I'm saying? Here's something so minor, yet you let it affect the other areas of your life that day. So you see how something major could just drag everything down. That's why we have to reach that high level of happiness in all five areas. That's why we need to set not just monetary goals, not just career goals or business goals, but goals in all those areas. Let's face it: your career is your life, your life is your career; they all intertwine, they all overlap. Unless you've got everything in balance, unless you've got everything at a high level of happiness, then you'll never really reach the success you want to reach.

When one of your five areas gets out of whack, it's going to drag the other four down with it. So you look to repair it. That's when you have to really start working hard in your life. It's easy to get everything in balance. It's harder to keep it in balance. That's when a person really has to start working hard on their life. You have to work hard on your life all the time. This doesn't come easy.

Success is not an easy thing, but I think when something gets out of whack, whether it be a family problem, an emotional problem, a physical problem, or a monetary problem, you have to sit down and start to work on it without sacrificing every other area of your life. Too many times, if someone's going through a bad business problem, they tend to forget their families and leave them out of the loop. They bring their troubles home with them, which is very natural. It's hard not to.

But in a situation like this, you should look to bring those people even more into the loop, because you need their support more than ever. If I were having a bad business problem, I wouldn't separate my family from it. I'd bring them into it, because maybe they could help me get through it, even just with their own emotional support.

In other words, instead of letting that one area that's out of whack drag down the other four, we're using the other four to try to prop that one area back up again to where it should be.

In order to create balance in our lives, we should be setting goals in all five of these areas of concentration. I don't want people to just set monetary goals. I don't want people to just set career goals. In order to create balance in your life, you have to set goals in all five of those areas. You have to set spiritual goals. You have to set emotional and physical goals and family goals. Everything intertwines. Everything overlaps everything else.

Let's face it: when we have a bad day at work, we bring it home with us. Or when we have a bad night or a bad day at home, we bring it to work with us. So if you don't think it overlaps, you're crazy. The whole idea is to set goals in each one of those five areas. Only by doing that can we finally define how we want our lives to look.

FOUR
The Five-Step Process

Now I want to take you through a five-step process that I've developed. It will help you to focus more clearly on what you want to achieve in your life, career, and business so that you will have the beginnings of your own personal, written five-year plan. This process will help you to focus in on what your goals are, what you want to achieve in your life and career, when you want to achieve it by, and how you're going to get to that point.

STEP ONE: SEE IT

The first step in this process is to be able to see it. You have to be able to see yourself successful, because if you can see yourself successful, you can be successful. If you can see yourself doing something in your mind, then you can do it. But if you can't even see yourself doing something in your mind, how can you possibly expect to be able to do it in reality?

Have you ever said to yourself, or have you ever heard anyone else say, "I can't imagine doing that in my wildest dreams"? Well, if you can't do it in your wildest dreams, what makes you think you can do it in real life? Because you know as well as I do that it's a lot easier to do stuff in our dreams. So see it. See yourself successful. Visualize it.

What you're trying to do is create a picture in your mind of what you want your success to be. We think in terms of pictures. We don't think in terms of words. We don't see numbers or words in our minds; we see pictures of what we want. And you're trying to create that picture of what you want your life to look like, of what you want your success to be. So see it, visualize it, and create that picture in your mind.

We all know people who are excuse makers—people that have a lot of what I call war stories. Those people always tell us how successful they could have been, but they never have any luck. They don't get any breaks. They don't have any connections. Nobody likes them. Everybody's always plotting against them.

In New York City we have a saying: "Everyone in New York knows somebody else who could have bought a building thirty years ago for $9." Have you known one of those guys? Have you ever walked down the street with one of those guys? If you have, you'd notice that they always say, "See that building over there?"

"Yeah."

"Thirty years ago I could have bought that building: NINE DOLLARS!"

"Well, why didn't you?"

"ARRGGHH, those lousy jerks, they talked me out of it."

"Why don't you buy it now?"

"Nah, it's too late now."

He's right. It *is* too late. For them it's too late because they believe it's too late.

But for a moment, let's say the excuse makers are right: they have no luck, never catch a break, nobody likes them, everybody's always plotting against them. I still have one question for all the excuse makers: how come you still could not even see yourself successful? Because, folks, nobody stops you from dreaming. And if you don't have good dreams, the only thing that's left is nightmares. So see it! See yourself successful. Visualize it. Create a picture of what you want your success to be in your mind.

As I travel around the world, one of the most distressing things I find is how few people I come in contact with who seem to be able to see themselves successful. Most the people I run into only have a capability, it seems, to see themselves failing.

I am sick and tired of people saying to me how bad business is. I am tired of salespeople saying stupid things like "Nobody's buying." Right. Nobody's buying. Absolutely. Nobody, anywhere, at any time is buying a single thing, at all, ever. Isn't that a stupid remark?

I know what you're thinking: that's not what they mean. Maybe not. But let me tell you this: you say something long enough, loud enough, and hard enough, and you start to believe it. Yes, I know it can be tough out there. Hey, I started my sales career in 1973, during one of the worst recesssions since the Great Depression. I don't care how tough it is, I don't care how tough it's ever been, and I don't care how tough it's ever going to be. Someone out there is always doing business, simply because they believe that they can. They see themselves successful.

So see it. See yourself successful. Visualize it. Create that picture of your own success in your mind. Once you've seen it, once you've visualized it, once you've created that picture in your mind, focus in on that picture. Focus in clearly until you can see every single detail of that picture, until you can take every single detail in that picture and describe it.

STEP TWO: WRITE IT DOWN

Once you've seen it, visualized it, focused on and described it down to its most minute detail, you are ready for step two of the goal-setting and planning process. Now that you can focus on and describe exactly what you see in your mind, you've got to write it down.

Did you ever wake up in the middle of the night with a good idea? What did you do?

You probably went back to sleep, and what happened? I'll bet you forgot all about it.

What happened if you wrote it down? The next morning you looked at the paper and reminded yourself, and you did something about it. You came up with some other ideas and wrote them down along next to it.

If we write the idea down, we get up in the morning, we see it, we get excited about it. But if we get an idea and go back to sleep, we wake up in the morning and forget it.

So, reason number one to write down your goals, very simply, is this: if you don't write them down, you're going to forget about them. Why else should you write down your goals? Because writing down a goal is your first commitment to doing it.

Let's face it: you have goals. You have dreams. And you know the big stuff? I mean the big stuff, the stuff you really want? Those big goals, those big dreams? You know as well as I do that those big ones could take you two, three, five, ten years of time, energy, and effort to achieve. If you're not willing to take ten minutes to write it down, what makes you think you're willing to take ten years of hard work, effort, and commitment to go out and get it?

The third reason to write them down is that writing down the goal makes you accountable to the one and only person that you can never fool: you. Let's be honest: you can fool anyone you want. You can fool your husband, you can fool your wife, your boss, your parents, your children, your teachers, your coworkers—you can fool anyone, except you can't fool yourself. You're the only one that knows the absolute, positive truth.

And once that goal is written, it's going to be really hard to look at yourself and admit you did nothing about going after it. But if it's not written, it's out of sight, out of mind. If it's not written, you don't have to admit you did nothing to go out and get it. That's why a lot of people don't write down their goals. They let themselves off the hook. If they don't write it down, they never have to admit they didn't do everything possible to get what they really, truly wanted out of their lives, and now they have the ability to complain about it.

So the first reason is that if you don't write it down, you forget it. The second reason: it's your first commitment to doing it. The third reason to write down your goals is it makes you accountable to the one and only person you cannot fool—which obviously is you.

Let me take it a step further, because I know lots of people in your life have told you to write down your goals, write down what you want, focus on and describe them. I'm sure you hear that all the time, and it goes in one ear and out the other.

See, I have a very strong belief, and that belief comes from working in the garment center. (You may wonder what strong beliefs could come from working in the garment center. I know there are a lot of guys still there that wonder.) Let me tell you what it is. I have found that no matter what you're selling in this world, the best way to sell it is to always make it as tangible as possible. I learned one thing: it's a lot easier to let people buy into what you're selling if you can let them touch and feel the merchandise, if you can make that sale as tangible as possible, no matter how intangible it is.

Let me show you a way that you can relate to in order to see why you should be writing down your goals.

Do you ever do the grocery shopping at home? I don't mean you single people, who buy a can of beer and a jar of mayonnaise. (You ever notice that? You open a single person's refrigerator, and the only thing in there is a can of beer and a jar of mayonnaise. It's true, it really is. I know; I was single for a lot of years.)

But if you do real food shopping on a regular or somewhat regular basis, have you ever gone with a list? And have you ever gone *without* a list? What's the difference? You don't buy what you need. When you go without the list, you forget stuff. You also buy more without the list. What else happens without the list? You waste time. What else do you waste? Money.

Listen to this. When you go out there without a list, you always end up wasting time. You end up wasting money. You go off in a million different directions. You take on a lot of things you don't need, and you don't seem to get what you want. Isn't that incredible?

Many people don't write down their goals. They always tell you, "I don't have time to sit down and start writing this stuff down. I've got to go. I've got to do. I'm just so busy. I've got a million things to do." They're always off in fourteen different directions. And when you go off in fourteen different directions at the same time, you never end up anywhere.

Do you know any of those people that are so busy but never get anything done? I call them human gerbils. Ever watch a gerbil? A gerbil is without a doubt the busiest little sucker in the entire world. He gets on that wheel, and he just goes whirring around, especially while you're sleeping. When he's done, he lies down on his side and starts panting because he's been so busy. Ever notice anything else? He never gets anywhere. He never gets off the wheel. He never leaves the cage.

Many people are like that. They're unwilling to take that one step back and invest that little bit of time up front to get that huge return in the back end. Isn't that incredible? Did you ever notice, when you go shopping with a shopping list, how focused you are? Did you ever notice how your shopping flows and you just go one aisle to the next? You flow through that store.

But when you go without a list, you always seem to be running from one end of the store to the next. It's amazing. You start out over here, you grab something, and you go, "Oh, geez, I forgot something." Then you have to go all the way to the other side of the store. You go, "Ah, man, I forgot something over there," and you're going, "Where'd I put my wagon?" Right?

Did you ever notice something else? Can you make up a shopping list by aisle? Sure. My wife can do that. You can do that. You make up your list, and you're visualizing where everything is in every aisle. What are you doing? You're seeing yourself successful.

Do you know why after you've made up that list by aisle, the shopping just breezes right through? Because you've already done it in your mind. It's not the first time you've gone that day; it's the second. The first time you did it, you did it in your mind. That's why it went so fast the second time. You already knew where everything was, because you'd already been there.

But when you go without the list, you always seem to buy the same things that you didn't need the last time you went without the list. Things like peanut butter, eggs, and milk.

Have you ever have a conversation with the peanut-butter shelf? You know what I'm talking about, because I know you've done it. Did you ever stand in front of the peanut-butter shelf saying to yourself, "I know I've got that at home. I know I have a jar. I'm sure we have peanut butter at home. No, I think we just ran out last week. No, I know we have it." People are walking by, wondering why this crazy person is talking to the peanut butter. You stand there for fifteen minutes debating whether you have peanut butter or not, and finally you go, "Oh, what the heck. I'll just buy another jar." You get home, and what happens? There are three jars in the cabinet from the other three conversations you had with the peanut-butter shelf.

Now let's take it a step further. I want to show you how, when we really focus and put together a sense of purpose and direction in our lives, it really comes back to us, how when we take that step back to take that little extra time to plan it out, we end up taking three steps forward or ten steps forward.

Let's look at what happens with a list, and without a list. Question: how long does it take you to write up your shopping list? Ten minutes?

How long does it take to do the shopping? I'm talking from the time you walk out the door of your house, get in your car, go to the supermarket, do the shopping, put the bags in the trunk of the car, get back in your car, drive home, unload the bags. An hour? An hour and a half? When you go without a list, how much time does it take you? How much time would you estimate you waste? A half hour? Thirty minutes extra. How much extra money do you blow when you go without the list? Let's say $50. That sounds pretty conservative.

In the larger scheme, shopping is irrelevant to the more important things in your life, yet look at this. When you're willing to take ten minutes up front to write down and plan out something as irrelevant as food shopping, within only an hour and a half you are saving yourself thirty minutes. Within an hour and a half, the willingness to take that ten minutes up front gets you a 300 percent return on your investment in time and puts $50 in your pocket that you didn't have.

Isn't that incredible? In something as irrelevant as grocery shopping. Could you imagine what kind of return you might get if you did that with your life and your career? That's why you write down your goals. That's why you take that step back to write it down and plan it out, which allows you to take those ten steps forward. If you want to be successful in life, you've got to be a long-range thinker. You can't think short-term.

Now that you know this, I want you to take out a clean sheet of paper. Draw a straight line across the top of the page, and on the right-hand side of the line write down today's date. On the left-hand side of the line, write down today's date minus five years.

want to see it happen. Because you know what? A goal is nothing more than a dream with a deadline. There are so many people out there who tell us all the great things they're going to do in their lives, but when we ask them when, they always say, "Sometime."

And you know as well as I do that *sometime* doesn't exist.

Let's face it. If you wanted to make an appointment to see me to sell me something, and you called up and said, "Warren, can I come over and see you sometime?" and I said, "Yes" and hung up, when would you come? You'd better do it right now, otherwise you have no idea when I'm going to be there.

Let's examine that word *sometime*. When do we use it? When we don't want to do something. Your wife asks you, "When are you going to paint that ceiling?" "I'll get around to painting that ceiling *sometime*." It's the same thing with *someday*. "*Someday* we're going to clean out this garage." "*Someday* I'm going to do this." And you know you have no intention of doing it. That's why you say *someday*, because *someday* never comes. We always use the word when we don't want these things to happen.

So what are we saying when we say we're going to reach our goals *sometime*? We're saying we have no intention of making them happen. So, time frames, folks, time frames. When you plug in what you want to see happen to you, plug in the year when you want to see it happen.

Number three is very important: Please don't place any limits on your ability to achieve. If it's what you really want, put it down. Don't rationalize your life away. Don't say, "This is what I really want, but I don't really believe I can get it, and since I don't really believe I can get it, I will settle for this." The second you say to yourself, "I will settle," that's as far as you're ever going to get, because you have just placed a glass ceiling over your head. You'll get as far as that glass ceiling. You'll spend the rest of your life looking through that glass ceiling at what you really wanted and saying, "I know I never could have gotten that, so I'm really kind of happy where I am now, and it's OK."

I don't believe in realistic goals. People say, "Set realistic goals." You know what that means to me ? To me, *realistic* is a code word for *low*. They're telling you, "Don't set a goal unless you're absolutely, positively sure you can achieve it. Don't even set a goal if you're not 100 percent sure you're not going to make it. Set your sights low. Don't set your sights too high. Don't ever try to stretch yourself. Be realistic."

People are always trying to prove me wrong. They say, "OK, you say I can have anything I want. I'll tell you what. Next year I want to make $10 million." Fine. What's so unrealistic about that? Haven't a lot of people in this world made $10 million in a year? Someone's doing it. In fact, more than someone's doing it.

The reality sets in when I tell you what you're going to have to do to get it. Then all of a sudden you'll say, "Oh, that's not realistic. Oh, no, I don't really think I need the $10 million." Sure—you don't want to do what it's going to take, because a goal is only realistic if you're willing to do what it takes to achieve it. It's not that it's not realistic.

It's not the goal or the dream that's realistic. It's what you're going to have to do to get it. Be specific, set time frames, and place no limits on your ability to achieve.

OK. Now plug in the most significant things you would like to see happen to you in the next five years. See yourself successful as you're writing these things down. Try to visualize it. Try to create a picture in your mind. It becomes a lot easier to be specific if you can think of it in a picture first.

Do you know what you've just done? You've made a commitment. What else did you do? You focused. You started the process. That's right: you set some goals.

I'm going to tell you something that might sound a little outlandish, but it's true. How long did it take you to do this? Ten minutes? The time it takes to make your shopping list. You've just done more than 99 percent of the people out there will ever do in their entire lives. That's unbelievable. That's scary. You've beat out 99 percent of your competition.

But all you've done is start the process. I always believe in starting slowly. I believe in making small changes. I'm not trying to preach the gospel to you. I'm not telling you that everything I'm saying is absolutely, positively right and that you must do it. But hopefully I'm going to give you a lot of good ideas.

If what you're doing is not working 100 percent to your satisfaction, here are some ideas. Give it a shot.

What have you got to lose? If what you're doing *is* working 100 percent to your satisfaction, hey, keep doing it. You'd be a dope to change it. But if what you're doing is not working 100 percent to your satisfaction and you're not willing to try some new ideas, then you know what? You do lose.

I'm trying to get you to have just a little different perspective—maybe a willingness to try something a little bit different. I don't want you to change overnight. I don't want you to change everything. You don't have to. I just want you to change a little bit, because I know that small changes, implemented on a regular basis, will always yield great results.

You don't need to start out as a goal-setting expert. I just want you to like this and be willing to try it, because if you like it and you're willing to try it, you'll keep doing it. And I know if you do it, it will work. But if you give up, then it's really over.

So let's start off slow. Go back over those goals you've written down and pick out three that you want to work on. Pick out three you want more than any others, and put a number one, a number two, and a number three next to them.

STEP THREE: PLAN IT OUT

We have just completed the second step of the five-step process. You've seen yourself successful, which was step one. You visualized it, created a picture, you focused on it, described it, you went to step two, and you wrote it down. Hopefully, you were specific, you put time frames on what you wanted, and you didn't place any limits on your ability to achieve.

Now you've set a destination for yourself. You've written down on a piece of paper something that says, "This is where I want to end up, and this is the time frame in which I want to get there."

Now we come to step three of the process. Step three says: what are you going to have to do to get from where you are now to where you want to be in the next one to five years? Step three very simply says you have to plan it out.

Everybody who has ever been successful has had a written plan. When generals send troops into battle, they always devise a written battle plan. A football coach sending a team out of the locker room spends an entire week putting together a written game plan for a game that lasts three hours, of which two hours are commercial breaks.

If you're in business for yourself, you have to have a written plan. In fact, the Small Business Administration of the United States will tell you that the single biggest reason small businesses fail is that they did not have a written business plan.

You've got to understand what the plan is. The plan is the piece of the puzzle that stops us from getting frustrated. The plan is the piece of the puzzle that helps us maintain the motivation every single day. People always ask me, "I set a goal for myself. It's five years down the road. How do I stay excited about it every single day?" Well, there's only one way to stay excited about it every single day, and that's to plan it out so that you can have something to look at every single day before you get to that goal.

Where are you now? You're right here. Where do you want to be? Why do you want to be there? There's your destination. There's your end result. Unless you put something in the middle here between where you are and where you want to be, all you're ever going to focus on is this end result. Every morning you're going to wake up, and the only thing you've given yourself to focus on is this end result. And every morning that you wake up and you focus on this end result and you're not there yet, what's going to happen? You'll get frustrated. Every day that you get frustrated, you get more frustrated. And the more frustrated you get, what's going to happen? You'll give up. And, as you know, the only time you fail is when you give up.

The plan is the roadmap, with the stopping-off points in between. It is nothing more than taking the big goal and breaking it down into little goals—breaking it down into something more realistic and closer to us that we can focus on every single day. Once we develop the plan with the stopping-off points, we're not focused on the end result every morning we wake up; we're only focused on the next step. The key is not to focus on the end result. The key is to focus on the process, on each one of those steps that we achieve. If we're focused on something that's really close and achievable, we're going to get it. When we get it, how are we going to feel? Great! And every day that we wake up and we feel great, what's going to happen? We're going to keep going! Let's face it: the fun is not in the being there. The fun is always in the getting there. The fun's in the process. The fun's in the fight.

Now I want to give you the three components that go into making up a successful plan: (1) a successful plan is expressed in continuous action; (2) a successful plan is broken down into accomplishable steps. (3) a successful plan always will give us the ability to measure our progress every step of the way.

Continuous action: Isn't it good to know what we have to do every single day? Isn't it great to know that before you come into work, you know exactly what you have to do that day to get you closer to what you want? Isn't it always so much easier to accomplish what you have to do that day when you know what it is, rather than leaving it open-ended?

Accomplishable steps are a big key to successfully implementing your plan. When you break your goal down to accomplishable steps, you're trying to do something that most people don't do. You're setting yourself up to succeed every day.

Most people set themselves up to fail every day. We always make it so hard on ourselves. What's that old expression? The toughest step of any journey is the first step. If the toughest one to take is the first one, why do so many people insist on making it the hardest one? Why not make it the easiest one? If you make the first step of your plan the easiest one to accomplish, won't that make it easier to take the step? Won't it take the fear out of that change?

The purpose of the first step is to just take it! Get moving. If you make it so easy to take, there will be no excuses not to do it. And if we take that first step and we accomplish it, how do we feel? We feel great! and if we feel great, what are we going to do next? Take another step. And if we keep taking those little small steps, we start to build up that habit and feeling of accomplishment. We're doing something every day that we absolutely, positively know we can do. We're setting ourselves up to succeed.

By setting ourselves up to succeed every single day, we're making ourselves feel better and better; we're starting to build confidence. Everybody's so worried about confidence. You can't be worried about confidence, because confidence doesn't come unless you do something. Confidence is a by-product of action. The commitment to the fact that we have to do something and want to do something gives us the courage to act. After we do it, we are confident in our ability to do it.

Have you ever skied? Remember the first time? Oh, man. You're standing up there at the top of the hill. Scared? Oh, yes. Why did you go down it? Peer pressure: your friends are standing at the bottom of the hill yelling, "Chicken!" Besides, did you ever notice that the T-bar only goes up? It doesn't go down. So you're standing at the top of the hill; you're scared. Do you have a lot of confidence in your ability at that point?

Absolutely not, but you go down anyway. When you get to the bottom of the hill, what do you say? "Wonderful!" What do you do at that point? You go right back up again. You aren't quite as scared the next time. You finally have some confidence, because you've done it.

The commitment to the fact that we have to do it and want to do it gives us the courage to go down the hill. It gives us the courage to act, and once we act, we start to feel confident in our ability to do it again.

That's why you make the first steps easy: so that you start to build confidence, to feel that you can accomplish anything. Because you start to feel you can accomplish anything, you're going to keep going. Once you start to feel great about the process, then increase the difficulty of the steps.

The best example I can think of came out of World War II: the North Africa campaign in 1943. Field Marshal Erwin Rommel had just obliterated an entire group of British and American forces in North Africa. He left in his wake two totally beaten and demoralized armies. So totally beaten and demoralized were these two armies that these men had no sense of self-worth. They had no confidence that they could do anything well. They not only felt lousy about themselves, they looked lousy. Their uniforms were filthy. The camp they were living in was filthy. They were a mess.

Into this situation came two men. At that point, General George Patton took over the American troops in North Africa, and Field Marshal Bernard Montgomery took over the British troops. These two men were as different as night and day, but interestingly, they were to immediately agree upon and institute the same policy.

What was the long-term goal? To win: of course! But if they left that as the only goal, could they do it? If they just got in front of those men and said, "Men, from now on, the only goal we're going to think about is winning. We've got to go out there and beat those guys," forget it. They weren't going to do it. Those soldiers didn't believe they could do anything.

The first thing they had to do was get these guys to believe that they could do and accomplish something; anything. So they set forth three criteria that these men had to meet every single day. They told these soldiers that they had to do these three things every day and these three things only.

"When you get up in the morning, you've got to wear a clean uniform. You have to do twenty push-ups every day, and you have to run one mile. That's it. That's all you've got to do."

It sounds so simple. But they knew if they gave these guys tasks that they could absolutely, positively do, how would they start to feel after a while? They'd feel good. They'd feel like they could conquer the world.

That's what happened. They started to feel better about themselves. Once you start to feel better about yourself, you start to look better. When you start to wear a clean, nice, fresh uniform, everything else around you starts to look better. All of a sudden, the camp got clean, because they didn't want to wear clean uniforms in a filthy camp. They started to believe that they could actually accomplish something, so now those two generals started to increase the tasks. And those men started to feel better, and better, and better, and finally they built themselves a lean, mean fighting machine. And, for those of you who don't know how it ended, we won.

You see what they did? They didn't ask people to do any more than they were capable of doing. They broke it down into accomplishable steps. Continuous action gave them the ability to measure their progress. When you give yourself the ability to see, touch, feel, and know that you're making progress, you start to feel good.

How many times do we set a five-year goal and give ourselves no ability to see, touch, or feel any progress? Three months into that goal, even though we've made normal, 5 percent progress—which is what we should have made—we have no way of knowing it, because we haven't given ourselves the ability to measure it. We say to ourselves, "Boy, you know, I've been working towards this goal for three months. I still feel like I'm on square one." Already you're getting frustrated.

Now you know that the plan should be expressed in continuous action and accomplishable steps, and should give you the ability to measure your progress every step of the way. I want you to take out three clean sheets of paper. At the very top of that first blank sheet of paper, write out whatever you designated as goal number one. Write out the goal in full at the top of that page, along with the year you intend to achieve it by.

When you're finished doing that, turn to the second page. Do the same thing with your goal number two: write out the goal in full at the top of the page, along with the year you intend to achieve it by. When you finish that, do the same thing with goal number three on the third page. Now, on each sheet, you have a goal written across the top of the page along with your time frame.

Go back to your first page and to your first goal. I want you to remember this: you cannot *do* a goal; you can only *work toward* a goal. Now list the steps you will take to achieve each one of these three goals.

See yourself successful. As you're writing down the steps that you will take to achieve each one of these three goals, try to visualize yourself actually doing it. Try to visualize yourself working towards these goals. Try to see yourself going through the process. Try to see yourself accomplishing those small steps. This is it, folks. This is the plan. Do it now.

STEP FOUR: ACT ON IT

OK. You have a plan: a roadmap. Amazing. You've got the beginnings of a true, written, specific five-year plan. You've finished the third step. You've got something very valuable that will work for you if you make it work. You've got a set of destinations for yourself, along with time frames. Hopefully, this road map will get you to the destinations that you set for yourself.

Now we come to step four. Step four is where the successful people will really start to separate themselves from everybody else. You've seen it, visualized it, created a picture, focused on and described it, set your goals, and planned it out. Step four, very simply, says you have to act. You've got to start. You've got to do something.

You have twenty-four hours to act on a good idea. If you do absolutely nothing about a good idea within twenty-four hours, that idea is dead. I'm not telling you that you have to do everything within twenty-four hours, but you have to take at least one action step. You've got to do something. Why? Because that's the only way you're going to keep the enthusiasm going.

Did you ever have a good idea? When did you get the most excited about it? When you first got it. If you don't do something about it right away, the enthusiasm starts to waver. A week later, you're not nearly as enthusiastic about it. Two weeks later, it's pretty much dead. If you don't do something—any little, tiny, action step every single day—you don't keep that enthusiasm going. You want to make this plan work? You've got to work it.

If you're used to setting goals, you might want to go beyond the three you've set. Take the rest of your goals and do the same thing. Put each one on a separate piece of paper. List the steps you'll take to achieve those goals. If you're not comfortable doing that, don't. Just stay with the three.

Remember—small changes, folks. I want you to do what's comfortable for you. I don't want you to break out of your comfort, because you don't need to. You just need to expand your comfort zone. I don't want you to get frustrated. I just want you to do a little bit more than you are used to. Take the goals you set, take the plans you've made, and rip them off that pad. Post them up somewhere where you can see them every single day. Because if you see them every single day, you're going to move toward them every single day. Remember things that sound dumb but are true? Out of sight, out of mind.

If you see that goal, if you see that plan up on the wall every single day, you're going to remember it. You're going to want it more every single day. You're going to move toward it every single day, and if you're not moving toward it, you're going to have to answer to that one person you can't fool, which is you.

We will always move toward our most dominant thoughts, so why don't we make our most dominant thoughts the things we want most out of our lives? If we put them up somewhere we can see them every day, we'll move toward them every day.

You should also be reviewing this plan on a consistent basis—at least every six months. Why? Your life changes. Your priorities change. Maybe what's a goal for you today might not seem that important to you six months from now. It's OK. It's yours. Cross it off. Get rid of it. You used a pen or a pencil and paper to write it; you didn't use a hammer and a chisel and a block of stone. If you've achieved all your goals, what do you do? SET SOME MORE!

What happens if you get to your deadline and you haven't achieved the goal yet? What do you do? Kill yourself? No. Move back the deadline. That's the beauty of this stuff. It's yours. Some people think that if they get to the deadline and they haven't achieved the goal, they've failed. "That's it. I failed." Believe me, the goal-setting police will not come to your house, kick down your door, and say, "You didn't get the goal. Come on, pal, you're coming with me. Goal-setting prison." It doesn't happen.

Some people are nuts. They set a goal: "By the end of the year, I want to lose thirty pounds. The end of the year comes, they've lost twenty-five pounds, and they say, "I failed." So you set a new goal: "I want to lose five pounds in three months."

It's yours. Do whatever you want with it, but it will only work to the degree that you make it work. But you've got to start. You've got to act. You've got to do something.

Most people talk about all the great things they're going to do with their lives. That's all they ever do. I have a friend who for years has been telling me he's going to start his own business. Every time he tells me, I ask him, "What kind of business are you going to be in?" because I love to hear the stupid story.

He says he's going to go into the mail-order business, Because he's one of those people who think that's easy. All you have to do is mail stuff out, and you sit, and people send you money. Good. Good. Every time I see him, I say, "How come you haven't started your business yet?" He says, "Well it's OK. I will. I'm just gathering information." After nine years of hearing that, I said to him, "You know, you're wrong. You shouldn't go into the mail-order business. You should open a library. You certainly have enough information."

You think he's ever going to do it? No way. He'll talk about it, he'll rationalize it, but he won't write it down, because if he writes it down, he's got to admit he's not doing it. You've got to act. You've got to start. You've got to do something.

I don't mean that you have to do something big every single day. What I mean is, do something, even if it's the tiniest, smallest action step. Even if all you do is something small, you maintain the habit, and by maintaining the habit, you maintain the enthusiasm.

Let me give you an example. I have a very good friend who decided about seven or eight months ago that he needed to get in shape. He wanted to create the habit of exercise in his life. And he decided that the only way to do it was to spend a full year working out every single day.

Now this guy does not go to a gym and run ten miles and work out on weight machines every single day. But he makes sure he does some sort of exercise at least once a day. He travels a lot, and he told me that even if it's 11:57 at night and he hasn't done anything that day, he'll get down on the floor and do ten sit-ups.

That's not what you'd call a heavy-duty workout, but you see what he's done? He's maintained the habit. Just by that little action, that tiny action of the ten sit-ups, he can say to himself, "I exercised today," and when he says to himself, "I exercised today," he says it with enthusiasm, because he takes great accomplishment in the fact that he did it again; he spent another day doing what he set out to do. He's so enthusiastic about it that there's no way he's not going to do it tomorrow. So it's not a matter of doing something big every day; it's doing something, no matter how small. It's just: do something.

Have you ever, in your entire life, have had at least one good idea? Did you ever have one of those ideas where you said to yourself, "You know, that would make a good book" or "That would make a great movie"? And did you ever sit with a friend of yours and say, "You know, this product could be incredible? If we ever got together, put some money behind it, and marketed it right, we could make millions." A year later, what happens? Somebody else did it. You say, "Hey, that was my idea."

Everybody walking the earth has had at least one good idea. But do you see the difference between a good idea and a successful idea? The difference is the successful ones did it. They acted.

I truly believe that there is no such thing as a bad idea. To me, the only bad ideas are (a) the ones that are not acted upon, and (b) the ones that are not acted upon properly. If you don't believe that there's no such thing as a bad idea, let me give you these four words: Teenage Mutant Ninja Turtles. Did you ever hear of a dumber idea than Teenage Mutant Ninja Turtles? I mean, that is the dumbest idea in the world.

For those of you that don't know what they are, let me tell you. These are little, green, crime-fighting turtles. They live in the sewer. Their boss is a rat, and they eat nothing but pizza. It is the dumbest idea in the world. But they have made movies, concerts, videos, cartoon shows, toys, games, books, comic books, clothing, etc. They have grossed billions of dollars, and it is the dumbest idea in the world.

But now let me ask you this. What if somebody came to you years ago and said, "I've got the greatest idea in the world! I'm going to make you rich beyond your wildest imagination. You got a pen? Good. This is what you've got to do: write me a check right now for $50,000. Give me a check; I'll make you a partner. Write me that check right now. Wait until you hear what it is. Wait until you hear what's going to make us so rich. Here it is, ready? Teenage Mutant Ninja Turtles! HAH! HAH! I know what you're thinking, but let me tell you what they are. These are little, green, crime-fighting turtles. They live in the sewer. Their boss is a rat, and they eat nothing but pizza. let me ask you, ARE YOU IN!?!?

What would you have said? "No, are you crazy?" You know who else said that? Hasbro. The number-one toymaker in the world. They said, "No one will ever buy little green turtles that live in the sewer."

Folks, there is no such thing as a bad idea, but you've got to start. You've got to act. You've got to do something.

STEP FIVE: STAY WITH IT

You've seen yourself successful. You've visualized it. You've kept that picture of success in your mind. You described it, right down to its most minute detail. You took that vision and you wrote it down; you set your goals. You were specific. You put a time frame on it. You did not place any limits on your ability to achieve. You took those goals, those destinations, and you planned them out. You expressed that plan in continuous options and broke it down into accomplishable steps, and gave yourself the ability to measure your progress every step of the way. You then took that plan and acted upon it. You took that first step.

Now we come to the fifth step of the goal setting and planning process. It's right here, at step number five, where the truly successful are going to break away from the pack. It's here where the 3 percent who will be great will leave the other 97 percent behind, because the fifth step of the process says you have to be able to sustain the effort. You've got to stay with it. It's called *persistence*.

People never fail. They just stop trying. As long as you keep going out there day after day after day after day, you are constantly giving yourself the opportunity to be successful, to be great, to be the best. But the second you stop, you have taken away any opportunity you ever had to be successful.

Yes, I know what'll happen. You know what'll happen. There will be roadblocks. There are always going to be roadblocks. Many of you have encountered some of those roadblocks already in your lives and your careers. But the choice is up to you. You can either sit around and wait for someone else to clear that roadblock for you, or you can go over it, around it, or through it, because no matter what you do, there will always be roadblocks.

Now I want to talk about a roadblock that I encountered. A lot of times, we hear about people in history who have done great things and some of the things they've overcome to do them. We hear about the Martin Luther Kings and the Abraham Lincolns and the Thomas Edisons. While those stories are all very inspirational and those people achieved great success and overcome tremendous obstacles, many people think, "That's all well and good, but I am never going to be Abraham

Lincoln, Martin Luther King Jr., or Thomas Edison. I can't relate."

Well, you can relate to me, because let me tell you something: I'm no different from you. And I am not crazy enough to believe that I've done anything with my life that anybody else couldn't do. The only difference between me and a lot of people is that I did it. So let me tell you about one of the roadblocks that happened to me in my career. Let me tell you how I handled it. Maybe next time when something like this happens to you—because we've all had something like this happen to us—you'll take a little different look at things, and maybe you'll handle it just that much better than you did the last time.

Christmas Eve, 1989. I went to the post office. I opened the post-office box, and there was a letter in there. It said I had been chosen to be one of the speakers at the Million Dollar Round Table conference in San Francisco the next June.

The Million Dollar Round Table is an organization based in Des Plaines, Illinois. It's in the life-insurance industry. To belong to it, usually you are one of the top 3 percent of all life-insurance producers in the entire world. To get into the organization, you have to qualify through your sales every year. To be a lifetime member, you have to qualify for something like ten years in a row.

Once a year, the Million Dollar Round Table holds its big annual conference somewhere in the United States. About 5000 or 6000 of the top insurance agents in the world show up. It's called "the world's greatest sales meeting." They choose their speakers very carefully. They put you through a rigid selection process. You have to submit a manuscript to tape. You have to audition. It is really rough, but it's a real honor to be chosen, because the Million Dollar Round Table can be a springboard for a speaker. It's almost like a comedian getting *The Tonight Show.*

Well, here I was. I'd only been a speaker for a little over three years, and I was being asked to speak at Million Dollar Round Table. When I read that letter, I let out such a yell that I woke up all the guys working in the post office.

I can't tell you how excited I was. The only thing that worried me was I had six months between then and that next June. I was worried I'd get so excited that I would explode into little pieces.

I decided I was not only going to do a good job, I was going to do a great job. I practiced that speech every single day. I knew it backwards, forwards, and sideways. I couldn't wait to get to San Francisco, not just to speak, but to get to meet all these people. Make some connections and hear some of the other speakers that they were bringing in.

I think I was the first one to arrive in San Francisco. I got there on Friday; the convention wasn't starting until Monday, and I wasn't speaking until the next Thursday. I went to sleep Friday night, woke up bright and early Saturday morning. Ran down to the speaker's lounge and registered. Got my packet. Went upstairs. Ripped open my packet and pulled it open, and there it was. My official Million Dollar Round Table program. This was a big deal for me. This was a real honor. It meant I was here.

I opened up the program, and I started to look through it. I came to the first section, which has little breakdowns of the different sessions and what's going to happen in each one. I started to read it to see which ones I wanted to go to. Then I came to mine: "The Three S's of Success, Warren Greshes." This was mine. It was a proud moment. It's always great to see your name in print. It's a real ego boost.

I started to read it. Here's what it said: "A challenge that many Million Dollar Round Table members feel is the need to show that corporate client a way of effectively rewarding a group of key employees." I said, "What's this? I didn't write this." And I kept reading. It said, "Look no further. John Picker will show you a unique yet proven method of combining split-dollar and deferred compensation concepts." I said, "What the heck is split-dollar? This is not mine. There's a misprint. This is from the session below. They did his twice. They left mine out." It was the only misprint in the book. I'm saying, "Oh, this is great. People are going to read this and they're going to say, 'Split-dollar; sounds boring. Forget this guy.' Great—my big chance. I'm going to be speaking in front of four boring guys.

Then I thought about it. I said, "Hold it. Don't get crazy. You're here. You've still got a shot. Besides, does anybody ever read this junk? Come on, whoever reads the program, right?" So I kept going. Then I came to the part with the speaker's pictures and bios. I said, "Wow,

me, and I looked at them and I said, "You know what, folks? What is really the worst thing that could happen to a speaker? To me, the worst thing is that after you're done, people just forget who you are. That's not going to happen here, folks. Because you know what? A year from now, you will not be sitting around saying, 'You know, I saw a speaker at Million Dollar Round Table. He was really good. Can't remember his name, but you know him. He's the guy whose picture *was* in the program.' Doesn't exactly narrow it down." But, I told them, "You might be sitting around a year from now saying, 'You know there was a speaker at Million Dollar Round Table. He was really good. I can't remember his name, but you remember that guy—he was the guy whose picture was *not* in the program.' Yes, Warren Greshes. That's me." I looked at that audience and I said, "And you know what else, folks? Any dope can get his picture in the program, but only one guy *can't*. I have done something no one else at this whole convention has done."

They gave me a standing ovation. They went absolutely crazy. The next day, it really started to happen. I was at a cocktail reception. People were walking up to me and saying, "You're Warren Greshes."

"I know that."

They said, "You know, everybody here is talking about you."

"Really?" By the way, folks, it doesn't matter what they're saying. It just matters that they're talking about you, because if they're talking about you, they're not talking about your competition.

"Yes. You're the guy whose picture's *not* in the program."

"Yes, that's me."

In fact, a guy walked right up to me in the hotel lobby and said, "You know, your picture really *isn't* in the program."

"Hello?" I said.

"No, no, no, you don't understand. That story was so good, I thought you had a phony program printed up and left your picture out on purpose, just to be able to tell that story."

Once the convention was over, it really started to happen. The people from the Million Dollar Round Table felt so bad about what had happened that the next January they ran a two-page article on me in their international magazine. Just goes to show you, folks, guilt can sometimes be a wonderful motivator.

And no more than two weeks after I got home, I started getting calls from all over the world: England, Wales, Ireland, Singapore, Malaysia, New Zealand, Canada, all over the United States. Everybody wanted to talk to and hire the guy whose picture was *not* in the program. It was incredible. Business was booming.

In fact, a few months after I had gotten home, a woman called me on the phone. She was another speaker at the Million Dollar Round Table. She called me up and she said, "I saw you speak. You were incredible." She said, "I am one of the cochairs for next year's National Speakers Association's annual convention in Palm Desert, California. How would you like to be one of the keynote speakers at the National Speakers Association's annual convention?"

"Let me check my schedule," I said. I put down the phone and I went, "Yes. I think I can make it." And you know what? A few months later, there I was in Palm Desert, California, on stage in front of some of the best speakers in the world.

Folks, the choice is up to you. You can either sit around and wait for someone else to clear that roadblock for you, or you can go over it, around it, or through it, because no matter what you do, there will always be roadblocks.

To me, life is not a sprint. Life is a marathon. That's the beauty of life. In order to be successful in a sprint, you have to flat-out win it. But in order to be successful in a marathon, all you have to do is finish. Right?

Do you know anyone who runs in marathons? Do you ever ask them if they won? Come on—no one ever wins those things. It's always some little guy from Ethiopia that wins. But aren't you always impressed when they told you that they finished? You know why? Because you see, anyone can finish a sprint. Anyone can last sixty yards, but not everyone has what it takes to go out there for twenty-six miles. The reason that all you have to do is finish in order to be successful is that most of your competition will drop out before that race ever ends. Most of the competition does not have what it takes to hang in there for twenty-six miles. Most of the competition does not have the commitment to go out there day after day after day after day, because they don't understand that success is not just a one-time thing.

Those of you who have been successful know that it is a lot easier to *get to be* successful than it is to *stay* successful. Most people will relax after that first taste of success, because they don't understand this: All the time, all the energy, all the effort, all the commitment that it takes to get to the top—that's the same thing you have to do every single day just to stay on top. Over the course of the marathon of life, you have to do those same things every single day.

For a number of years, I've been carrying around this newspaper article. It's now yellow. It's from the front page of *The New York Times*. It's the obituary of a truly amazing man. His name was Jascha Heifetz. He was considered the greatest violinist of all time.

The obituary describes him this way: "Jascha Heifetz, the violinist whose name for more than half a century was synonymous with perfection of technique and musicianship." Can you imagine? This man was considered the very best at what he did for more than fifty years in a row Can you imagine being the best at what you do for more than fifty years in a row?

The obit said that it amused him that people expressed surprise that he still needed to practice after fifty years of being the best. Do you know that even after fifty years of being a professional, Jascha Heifetz practiced three hours every day? Do you know what he did to start every day? Scales. Something he knew how to do when he was only three years old. Yet here he was, fifty years of being the best, practicing three hours every day, doing scales.

I said, "Why?" I said. "This guy's already the best. Why is he doing that every day?"

Because, you see, Jascha Heifetz understood. He knew everything he had to do. All that time, all that energy, all that effort, all that commitment that he had to put forth to get to be the best—that was the same thing he had to do every single day just to stay the best.

There was a quote from him. He said, "If I don't practice for one day, I know it. If I miss two days, the critics know it. But if I miss three days, my audience knows it."

You know what, folks? Your audience knows it too. That's right. They know when you don't feel like being there that day. They know when you didn't feel like getting out of bed in the morning. They know when you don't believe in who you are or what you do, and they know when you don't believe in the products and services that you sell. None of us can act that well. If we could, we'd all be heading out on the next plane for Hollywood to accept an Academy Award.

Commitment is not something you're born with. It's something you acquire through setting goals, planning, and having a sense of purpose. It's something that has to be developed. You cannot be born with a burning desire to be the best. There's got to be a reason. You've got to be committed to something. You have to decide. What are you committed to?

I want to end with a story of a man who had that commitment, who had that burning desire. It was lucky for him that he had it, because this man had little or nothing else. He had no job. He had no money. He had a family to support, but he also had that burning desire, and the one thing he wanted was to work. He was willing to do any kind of job. He looked everywhere and every day, but he just couldn't connect. As a last resort, he went to see his parish priest. He sat down with him and he said, "Father, please can you help me? I want to work. I'll do any kind of job. Can you help me find a job?" The father looked at him and he said, "You know, I'm glad you came, because I can help you and I will. My best friend is the president of New York University. I'll give you a letter of recommendation. Take it. Go see him. I think he can help you find a job."

The man is thrilled. He takes this letter, heads down to NYU, and sits down with the president. He shows him his letter and tells him his story: he's out of work, he's got no money, he's got a family to support. The president reads the letter, looks at the man, and says, "I'm glad you came. I'm glad the father sent you, because I can help you and I will. I'm going to give you a job right here at NYU. I'm going to make you the head janitor right here at NYU."

The man is ecstatic. He says, "That's great. Can I start today?"

"Sure, but please, as a formality, would you please fill out this work application?"

The man looks at him and says, "Sorry, I can't. You see, I can't read or write."

The president of the school looks up and says, "Wow. Now we have a problem. You must understand. I'm the president of a major university. How would it look if I started to hire people who can't read or write? I'm terribly sorry."

This guy's devastated. He gets up to leave. As he's walking out the door, the president says, "Wait, please. I hate to see you leave empty-handed. Here, take this." It's a box of cigars. He says, "I don't want them. I don't smoke." The president says, "They're brand-new. The wrappers are still on them. Please take them."

The man takes the cigars, leaves, and starts to wander the streets. He ends up in downtown Manhattan, on Wall Street in the financial district, standing all alone on a street corner with a box of cigars under his arm. All of a sudden, he looks up, and across the street he sees a cigar store. He gets an idea. He says, "You know what? I'll go in there, and I'll sell that store owner my box of cigars. At least I can make some money."

So he goes into the store. He shows the owner his box of cigars. He says, "Look, the box is brand-new. The wrapper's still on it. I'm out of work. I have no money. I have a family to support. Would you please buy the box?" The store owner looks at him and says, "Look, I'd love to help, but I can't. Understand, I've been a reputable store owner here for twenty years. How would it look to my customers if I started buying cigars off the street? I'm terribly sorry, but I'll tell you what you could do. There are a lot of people walking around this area that have money in their pockets. Why don't you make up a sign, go a few blocks down, and sell the cigars for $1 apiece?"

"You think I could?" the man says.

"Well, you could try."

"Would you help me? I can't read or write. Would you make up the sign for me?"

The cigar-store owner says, "Sure."

So he makes him a sign. The guy takes the sign, he takes the cigars, goes a few blocks down, he puts up the sign, he puts out the cigars, and in two hours he sells every single cigar.

He's got $20. He gets another idea. He says, "You know what? I'm going to take this money and buy two boxes of cigars." So he buys the two boxes. He sells those, he takes that money, he buys four boxes, he sells those. He goes, "Whoa. This is great. I'm coming back tomorrow."

Well, he came back tomorrow. Understand this: this was a man of commitment, desire, and action. While he might not have possessed the highest level of education, commitment, desire, and action have nothing to do with education. He was back there that next day, and day after day, week after week, month after month, year after year, he's down on that corner selling cigars. He's out there for FIVE YEARS selling these cigars! It doesn't matter if it's hot, cold, sunny, windy, snowing, raining—he's out there for five years.

Finally, he decides to get in out of the rain. He gets another idea. He says, "You know what? I'm going to buy that cigar store."

So he approaches the owner and tells him the whole story of the cigars and the corner and the five years and the wind, rain, and snow, and says he wants to buy the store. Is he willing to sell? The man says, "You know what? I've been here for twenty-five years now. I'm ready to retire. I'll sell you my store."

"How much do you want?"

"I want $1 million."

"Wow, that's a lot of money. Where am I going to get $1 million?"

"Why don't you go to a bank and take out a loan?"

He says, "Do you think I could?"

The store owner says, "You could ask."

The man goes to the bank. He sits down with a loan officer, and he tells him the story about the cigars and the $1 apiece and the five years and the store and the wind and the rain and the snow. He says he wants to buy the store, and he needs a loan.

The loan officer says, "How much do you need?"

"I need a $1 million."

"You know, that's a pretty big loan. Do you have any collateral?"

The man looks at him and says, "Collateral? What's that? Look, you don't understand. I can't even read or write. What's collateral?"

"Do you have any money?"

"Yes, I have money. In fact, I keep my money in this bank. I don't know how much I have, but here's the bank-book."

This loan officer opens this bankbook, and his hands start shaking and his eyes pop right out of his head. He looks up at this man and says, "You have $465,000 in this bank—$465,000? From selling cigars on a corner for five years? Sir, you are a financial genius, and you can't even read or write. Have you any idea where you would be if you could read and write?"

The man says, "Yes. I'd be the head janitor at NYU."